NEVER PUT AN ALLIGATOR IN YOUR CAR

LIFE LESSONS FOR CHILDREN OF ALL AGES

BETH DETJENS

CONTENTS

Acknowledgments   v

Introduction   vii

1. Never Put an Alligator in Your Car   1
2. Baque: Part One   8
3. Tippytoes   20
4. Harriet   29
5. Zipper   38
6. George & Emily   46
7. Fatunia & Petunia   56
8. Boomer   68
9. Pumpkin   76
10. The Horse: Part One   80
11. Angel   89
    Epilogue   95

ACKNOWLEDGMENTS

In many ways, this book is a cautionary tale, because leading with our hearts instead of our heads could have ended in disaster—and sometimes did. To be clear, I do not recommend removing wildlife from their natural habitat unless it is within the legal and humane confines of organized animal rescue operations.

I am so incredibly grateful for both my childhood and adult family. I love you more than words can say. These books exist because of my husband's and kids' unwavering support – and because of my original family, whom you are about to meet. Thank you for the most wonderful childhood a kid could ask for.

Thank you, first and foremost to my mom, who

is *the* most loving, patient and wise person I know. You went along with our crazy ideas, but you made sure we all learned as much as possible from them. I'm glad you put your foot down when reason forsook everyone else in the family.

Thank you to my beautiful and loving sister, who was so often the voice of reason that kept us grounded. There is no one else I would have chosen to share our childhood with.

Last, but most definitely not least, thank you, Dad, for your fearless dedication to animal welfare and for the once-in-a-lifetime opportunities you brought into our lives. Your intelligence, intuition, and instincts kept us all relatively safe and allowed us to save countless lives. You taught us so much about animal care — and about helping others. You showed me that everyone is worth saving and the most important people to help are those who can't return the favor.

I would also like to thank my talented and insightful editor, Liam, for helping me craft these stories into a cohesive narrative that shines the light on some simple yet profound truths to live by. Thank you.

I hope you enjoy reading these stories as much as my family enjoyed living them.

INTRODUCTION

Before I tell you about our family's menagerie of unusual pets, I guess I should tell you about my family. If you already read my first book, *Never Buy a Raccoon at a Gas Station: Life Lessons for Children of All Ages*, then you will already know a lot of this. If you haven't read my first book, I highly recommend you do. It's all about our pet raccoon, Bandit —his hilarious adventures and some of the lessons we learned from him.

This book is a bit broader in scope, encompassing some of my dad's weird childhood pets, along with several different varieties of wild and wacky pets from my own childhood. You see, I'm a third-generation animal enthusiast. Both my dad and his dad carried the gene. They both had pet alligators as young boys, both loved all kinds of animals, and both passed it on to their children.

When I was a kid, our small farm in rural Virginia was home to any and every animal in need. Both Mom and Dad were school teachers, and Dad was also a pastor, so we had summer vacations together, as well as snow days and any school holidays. It made us a close family, full of laughter, love — and of course — animals.

Everyone in our family loved animals. Mom and my older sister appreciated animals at a distance, while Dad and I loved them up close and personal. At any given time, we had two dogs and any number of more interesting animals. Life at our house was never ever boring.

Through the years, we had traditional pets like dogs, cats, hamsters, rabbits, fish, birds, but we also had more uncommon pets. We had wildlife, including a raccoon, deer, opossum, skunk, white squirrel, flying squirrel, snakes, silver foxes, and more. We had farm animals, including riding horses, miniature horses, milk goats, pygmy goats, cows, African pygmy pigs, and more. And we had exotic pets, including alpacas, ostriches, South American leopards, and more.

You might be surprised to learn that, at least at the time these stories happened, it was (usually) perfectly legal to permanently care for rescued wildlife and to raise exotic pets like ostriches and alpacas — especially in rural Virginia where we lived on almost eight acres of land.

Our local veterinarian was able and willing to help with the miniature horses, goats and pigs. For any kind of wildlife or more exotic animals, however, we were essentially on our own. We did our own vaccinations, deworming, deliveries, first aid, and even some surgeries.

Dad has always had an uncanny ability to learn new skills, almost exclusively by instinct. I always loved watching him figure out a solution and then execute it with stunning success, almost every single time. Even when it seemed nothing could be done — especially when it seemed nothing could be done — he would come up with some crazy idea, and it would work.

Life was certainly an adventure with all of those animals. We never knew what animal Dad would come home with next, and each day was a new surprise.

Perhaps the best way to set the stage for the crazy cast of characters you're about to meet is to tell you a story from my dad's childhood. Perhaps because his dad had a pet alligator as a boy, or perhaps because he just wanted one, Dad decided he should have a pet alligator. I believe he was between five and ten years old at the time, and his family lived very near the banks of the Carrabelle River, in the Panhandle of Florida.

I never heard the part of the story that explained how or where he found the baby alligator, but he acquired an alligator and somehow convinced his parents to let him keep it. I'm sure they figured he'd quickly lose interest or the alligator would escape in a matter of days, but they were wrong. That alligator stayed around long enough to become a full-grown adult alligator. Dad liked to walk it around on a leash, and it was relatively tame—or at least as tame as an alligator can be expected to be.

Around the time his alligator, Allie, reached adulthood, Dad also had a litter of puppies that his pet dog unexpectedly had. The puppies and their mother were in a comfy outdoor kennel in the shady part of the back yard, and Dad visited his puppies all throughout the day, taking great care of them. He had picked out his favorite puppy, the one that he would be allowed to keep when the others all found loving homes. It was a small, fluffy, brown-and-white puppy with a curly tail.

One afternoon when Dad came home from school and went to check on his puppies and his alligator (who now roamed freely), he was surprised to hear frantic barking. All of the puppies and the mother were barking constantly. As he got closer, he heard a hissing noise. He knew what that was, so he dropped his schoolbooks and ran full speed toward the kennel.

What he saw stopped him in his tracks. The kennel door was open, and Allie's body was halfway inside the kennel—his mouth wide open as he hissed menacingly at the puppies. Even worse, the puppy who was barking almost nose to nose with Allie was Dad's favorite puppy.

He did the only thing he could think of. He grabbed a broom that was propped up near the wall of the kennel and gave a good smack on Allie's back to divert his attention from the puppies. Over and over he lowered the broom on Allie, screaming for him to "leave my puppies alone." None of the blows seemed to have much effect on Allie, but one must have found its mark. Allie suddenly grew still just as his jaws were within striking distance of Dad's favorite puppy.

By this time, Dad's mom had heard the commotion in the backyard, and she had leaned out of one of the upstairs windows of the house for a better look. She saw an alligator inside a dog kennel, dogs barking like crazy, Dad wildly swinging a broom, and, by now, screaming, "I've killed him! I've killed my alligator!" He was crying and screaming, and Allie did seem to be gone.

She finally convinced him to come inside "right this very minute," but only after he had drug Allie's still body out of the kennel and securely latched the door behind him, with all of the puppies safely inside.

I don't know how long he was inside the house, but when he came back outside to bury his pet alligator, there was no alligator. Allie was gone! Years later, there were stories of an enormous alligator that was repeatedly sighted near that river, and Dad always wondered if that was Allie. If so, Allie lived a very long and happy life—at least when he recovered from missing his lunch that day.

And what's the point of telling you this story? More than just the fun of a good story, Dad's first exotic pet helps explain some of the wild and wonderful animals he brought into our lives from that day on. Needless to say, it would take a lot more than that close call with Allie to keep him on the domestic side of pet ownership.

NEVER PUT AN ALLIGATOR IN YOUR CAR

When most people see an alligator on the side of the road, they keep driving. Dad was not like most people. When he saw anything, dead or alive, on the side of the road, our family protocol dictated that we stop and check to see if the injured animal needed our help. That's exactly how we'd rescued a skunk, opossum, snakes and a host of other animals.

One summer day, my family was out for a Sunday afternoon drive on the backroads of Florida's Panhandle, which was home at that time. This fateful day was a year or so before I was born, so I had to hear this story from the survivors. The family car was a 1969 powder blue Chevy Nova. In the front seat were my dad and mom, with my older sister, Lora, in the back seat. Dad was driving, and the windows were down, thanks to no air conditioning in the car. The black leather seats in the car only amplified the Florida heat, and the windows were down to make it almost bearable. The open windows brought in the smells of the sandy road, the scrub oaks and the pines as they drove for miles and miles without seeing another car.

Long drives through the Florida Panhandle were a family favorite, especially on Sunday afternoons. During this particular family drive, they had seen an alligator lying on the side of the road completely still and apparently hit by a car. This was before the time of seat belts, so Lora – who was three at the time – was perched on the edge of the back seat, right in the middle, with her arms folded on the middle of the front bench seat back and her chin resting on her folded arms so she could see out the front better.

I'm not sure who spotted the alligator first, but as soon as Dad saw it, he was determined to get a closer look. Having had a pet alligator as a young boy, Dad had a soft spot for alligators and immediately decided he should try to save it if it could be saved. He pulled the car over as far as he dared on the soft, sandy shoulder of the narrow road. As far as the eye could see, the road was lined on both sides by tall pine trees, with not a soul in sight. The treetops rustled with squirrels and random birds whose voices created a soft but steady soundtrack in the background.

Dad carefully approached the alligator, ready for any sudden movement. He wasn't surprised when he was able to walk all the way up to the alligator's head without any hint of movement. Daring to inch even closer, he checked for a pulse and felt nothing. Was it the toughness of the alligator's skin, or was there really no pulse? After a few more minutes of careful examination, Dad announced with finality that the alligator was indeed dead.

He decided its death should at least serve a purpose. In Florida, alligator was just another white meat, and Dad was looking forward to a tasty alligator stew, and possibly some amateur taxidermy, a belt or some boots. At any rate, that alligator was coming home with them.

Dad hefted the 5-foot-alligator into his arms as best he could and lumbered over to the car with him, calling for Mom to open the car door. Mom promptly replied, "You are not putting an alligator in this car." Dad's solution to Mom's fear was to put the alligator in the back seat so she wouldn't be scared of it. There was just one problem. The back seat was already occupied—by my 3-year-old sister. Mom and Dad reached a quick compromise in which Lora joined them in the front seat, and the alligator would ride as far away from them as possible, in the rear window of the sedan. For those of you too young to remember, back seats at that time were a solid bench with no arm rests or cupholders or anything but the bench and a flat ledge, or shelf, above it. The rear window ledge was a flat surface that ran the width of the car, wide enough to hold small items—or in this case, a full-grown alligator.

Mom suggested the trunk of the car, but Dad didn't want it to overheat and spoil the meat. So, off they went with the alligator in the rear window. Mom's eyes were focused on Lora and the alligator, determined to keep them separate no matter what. Dad turned on the radio to lighten the mood, reminding them that they would be home in just a few minutes.

They hadn't gotten very far when Mom whispered for Dad to pull over. He insisted they were almost home and needed to hurry so he could get a closer look at his find. Mom had already gotten a pretty close look from the front seat and didn't like what she was seeing. She said the alligator's eyes had opened, but Dad reassured her that it was just part of rigormortis and that the alligator was definitely dead.

Against her better judgment, Mom agreed but edged closer toward the windshield, putting as much distance between the alligator and Lora as possible. Another minute or so passed, and then the quiet tension in the car was shattered by Mom's ear-piercing scream. Dad turned to see what was the matter and came almost face-to-face with the alligator, which had, in one motion, whipped its body down from the window ledge and onto the floorboard, just one jaw's snap away from all three of them.

By this time, Mom was in full-on panic, clutching Lora to her chest as they crouched in the floor of the front seat (before the days of mandatory seat belts in cars). Dad slammed on the brakes to disorient the alligator and, of course, to stop the car. He did indeed disorient the alligator as it crashed into the back of the front bench seat, but he also tossed the three of them around the front seat like rag dolls. Now that the alligator was on the floorboard of the backseat, Mom and Lora were in full-on panic mode.

In the same instant the car stopped, Dad jumped out and opened the back car door. The alligator was trying to come over the front seat, and Mom had rolled out of the car with Lora, where she kept screaming. I would have, too.

Dad closed the front door to force the alligator out the back door and, thankfully, the alligator took the hint. As soon as he saw the open door, he bolted as fast as he could move and darted right into the underbrush. He didn't even glance in Mom's and Lora's direction. Dad was on the other side of the car, yelling for them to get back in and close the doors in case the alligator changed his mind.

I don't know if the alligator got fed up with the talk of alligator stew and boots, or if the effects of shock had simply worn off, but something highly motivated him to get out of our car and fast. That was the first and last day that any of us ever put an alligator in the car.

ALLIE'S Lesson: That 5-foot-long alligator, known in later years as Allie, taught us an important lesson the day Dad lifted him into the rear window of the family sedan. When he put it in the back seat of the car with my sister, his plans included an alligator belt, boots, maybe an amateur venture into taxidermy, who really knows? His plans most certainly did not include what happened.

It all must have seemed like déjà vu to Dad, who had been fooled not once, but twice, by seemingly dead alligators. His pet alligator as a child (Allie I) disappeared after Dad ran away thinking he was dead, only to resurface years later as an enormous alligator just down the river from the scene of his supposed death. I later learned that this form of shock isn't uncommon in reptiles. A good lesson to learn if you ever are tempted to put an alligator in your car....

2

BAQUE: PART ONE

I t was a typical steamy afternoon in the Amazon River Basin, in a sleepy little town called Rurrenabaque. The rain pounded relentlessly on the roof of the adobe mission house, which was tucked under the spreading branches of an acai tree beside the Beni River, which was flowing furiously toward the Amazon River.

For as long as I can remember, Dad has always taken an afternoon nap every day. Every. Single. Day. As is common in many Latin American countries, the whole town pretty much shut down from roughly 11am until 2 o'clock in the afternoon. This daily siesta was among the things Dad loved best about spending time in Bolivia.

At this time, I was in middle school, my sister Lora was in high school, and my parents were both still teachers. Dad took a good portion of each summer vacation to serve as an independent missionary in Bolivia, which is where he was when he met Baque.

He had lived in La Paz for a year in his 20s as a schoolteacher, but doctors then had told him the high altitude would shorten his lifespan by decades. So, he had lived his 30s, 40s, and 50s in the United States, spending several summers in the Amazon River Basin of Bolivia. The low elevation, pure air, and nutrient-dense vegetation of the rainforest proved highly beneficial to his health. Over that time, he was able to build a church, a houseboat for a local pastor to preach from (at a safe distance from the hostile tribes along the Bene River), a radio station, a television station, an orphanage, a feeding center, and more. This story happened when Dad was in his 50s and spending summers in Bolivia.

It was the people of Bolivia who had drawn Dad there, but he was fascinated by the local wildlife, which was prolific in the small jungle village where he lived. He had a monkey, a scarlet macaw, a three-toed tree sloth, massive snakes, and many other jungle creatures. The animal that had most captured his attention and affection, though, was a small leopard species called the Geoffroy's Cat, which was similar to an ocelot but looked more like a leopard. He was convinced that a hybrid cross of the Geoffroy's Cat and a domestic tabby cat would make an ideal pet, and he had decided to name the new hybrid breed the "Painted Amazon Cat."

An avid napper, Dad resented few things more than being awakened from a good nap, but the knock at the door of Dad's mission house sounded urgent enough to wake him from a sound sleep. Grappling for his glasses, he stumbled out of bed and to the door.

The sight on his doorstep momentarily stunned him into silence. A small boy and his father stood nervously in the doorway, barefoot and muddy from the rain, holding out a small bundle that moved ever so slightly.

Dad had a keen eye for interesting animals and especially for animals in need. He guessed that whatever was squirming in the dirty t-shirt the boy held was both interesting and in need. He was right.

Sensing the need, Dad quickly accepted the

bundle and moved the fabric away to see a tiny, wet Geoffroy's Cat staring back at him. In true Geoffroy's Cat form, the cub stood up on its hind legs, using its tail for balance, showing off the impressive rosette spotting pattern for which Geoffroy's Cats are known. The father's hand was still extended, awaiting his finder's fee. Dad reached in his pocket, provided the expected amount and retreated to the sofa to get a closer look at his new pet, which he quickly named "Baque" as a shortened form of his home village.

Though Baque's fur was soaking wet, it was easy to see the black bands around the legs, the large rounded ears with white tufts of fur inside, and the most beautiful spotting pattern Dad had seen yet. This was definitely the perfect sire for his first litter of Painted Amazon Cats.

Most of the other cats the villagers had brought to him for consideration were already hybrids of one variety or another, and few had retained enough of the coloration and leopard-like traits he sought. But Baque was simply stunning. After a little sugar water, eggs and other nutrients Dad kept handy, Baque was dry and fluffy, and ready to explore his new home.

The father had explained that he'd heard Dad

was looking for spotted cats and that he had found this orphaned spotted cub in the jungle. Knowing that his travel plans would soon take him back to the United States, Dad decided the cub would need to come with him as soon as Baque was strong enough to travel—and as soon as the veterinarian (closest one was a 24-hour drive away in La Paz) signed off on the paperwork.

At that time, Baque was likely only days or weeks old and had to be fed often and carefully. Dad kept him close in a bright green vented bread basket with a domed lid on top. About the size of a deflated soccer ball, it was just the right size for such a tiny cub, and he stayed cozy in his covers when it was time to nap or at bedtime. The rest of the time he was with Dad.

Finally, it was time for Dad and Baque to make the trip to La Paz for some vaccinations and a health certificate so he could travel with Dad home to the United States. So, they set out for La Paz, a 24-hour bus ride up from the Amazon rainforest on the Yungas Road, which was affectionately (and aptly) nicknamed the "Road of Death" due to the hundreds of fatalities each year. In 1995, the Yungas Road officially earned the title "world's most dangerous road"—due in part to armed robberies along the way, but mostly due to so many busloads of passengers toppling off the side of the mountain.

A local vet was happy to check Baque out , and Dad filed all the proper paperwork to legally import this beautiful baby Geoffroy's Cat. Once the flight home was booked, they set out to the airport and they were off.

The only hitch at the airport was when Dad realized that a cargo hold was no place for a fragile leopard cub. He would have to make sure that Baque stayed in the cabin with him. But how? Just then, he noticed an elderly woman carrying a green bread basket just like the one Baque was in, cradled in Dad's arms under a jacket for extra warmth.

That was it! He'd carry Baque in the bread basket right onto the plane to spare him the trauma of the cargo hold. Lots of other passengers carried food in similar bread baskets for the long, 12-hour flight; he had even placed the basket on the ticket counter in the airport to show off the beautiful cub—and his legal documentation— without a single raised eyebrow. Both Dad and Baque made it safely home with no issues at all. This is a great time to say, "don't try this at home" as many of Dad's impulse decisions were question-able at best.

When we picked Dad up at the airport, we had no idea he was bringing home an exotic cat. Even Mom didn't know, but she was used to Dad's animal surprises and took it in stride with barely a raised eyebrow. While Lora and I fawned over Baque, Dad explained that he was a South American Leopard, also known as a Geoffroy's Cat, and that he would grow to be almost twice as big as a house cat and would look just like a leopard. He explained his plans for creating a new hybrid breed, his Painted Amazon Cats, and we quickly reminded him that both Lora and I were allergic to cats. He assured us we'd be fine with Baque because he wasn't a domestic cat.

I'll never know how in the world he knew (or guessed) that, but he was right. I couldn't be in a room where a domestic cat had been without my throat closing up, but I'd been holding Baque for several minutes without even a tickle in my throat from allergies. Lora was fine, too. In later years, a study published in the Journal of Allergy and Clinical Immunology concluded that people with an allergy to cats showed a significantly weaker response to big-cat dander—likely due to the fact that big cats secrete a lesser amount of the single protein that triggers allergies. The 1990 study tested the dander of eight species of felines, including ocelots, pumas, servals, Siberian tigers, lions, jaguars, snow leopards, and caracals (desert lynx).

So, it was settled. Baque would live in the house with us—our first indoor housecat—and Dad would build him a small indoor habitat for extra comfort. Thankfully, Mom put her foot down on an actual habitat in our living room, so Dad settled for palm trees Baque could climb.

Picture for a moment our living room. Our house was an average size, with a river rock fireplace, large plate-glass windows, and red cedar walls facing a mountain view. Nowhere in this room—or state, for that matter—did it make sense to have palm trees. Also, where in the world were we going to get palm trees in Virginia?

Dad decided he could make artificial palm trees by spray-painting palmetto fronds the right shade of green and sticking them into the top of a cut off palm tree trunk, which he would then anchor in a bed of Spanish moss inside a red cedar box that he built to be the sturdy base for each of the palm trees. The result was surprisingly attractive and lasted for many years.

He placed the artificial palm trees in the corners of the room and behind the couch so Baque had a place up high to lounge in, pounce from, and just take in his treetop view. It was glorious—for Baque. He would sit in the top of a tree behind the couch and wait until everyone was settled in, the room was quiet, and you'd forgotten he was even in the room. And then he'd pounce down from the tree to the top of your head, your lap, or beside you on the couch. It was especially startling for our guests—especially if we'd forgotten to tell them we had a South American Leopard Cat. I think we sometimes forgot to tell them half-on-purpose so that we could all enjoy the surprise.

As much as Baque liked to jump down from high places, he also liked to jump up from low places. His favorite greeting when we came home from school was a series of leaps across the room, ending with one giant leap from the floor to about your waist, and then one more leap from your waist up to your shoulder. He would ride around that way, just like our pet raccoon Bandit had done years earlier. Guests weren't particularly fond of that greeting either. Baque, however, didn't seem to care.

By the time he was grown, Baque was almost twice the size of housecat, but he was as gentle as a lamb. As a wild cat, he had several advantages compared to domestic cats. In addition to not triggering our cat allergies, Baque also lacked the negative personality traits cats are known for. Specifically, he was not aloof and independent. He loved being with us and loved to play—like a dog actually. He acted more like a dog than our actual dogs sometimes. He would play fetch with toys, come to us when we called him, and was housetrained. He was awesome!

And then, one day, the phone rang. Dad's contacts in the cat breeding program had been helping him find other South American Leopard Cats that he could add to the hybrid breeding program as other sires. As part of the sharing process, he had circulated pictures of Baque to illustrate the type of spotting and coloration that he needed.

The phone call was from an exotic cats breeder in Louisiana* who was licensed to house all sorts of big cats, including tigers. Dad thought he was calling to tell him he'd found more Geoffroy's Cats, but he was calling for another reason. Someone helping Dad find cats had shown Baque's picture to this man, and he immediately recognized that Baque wasn't a Geoffroy's Cat, as the Bolivian vet had listed him. Baque was a margay.

At that time, margays were on the endangered species list, and unauthorized possession of a margay carried a long prison term and massive fine. To be fair, a margay looks almost exactly like a Geoffroy's Cat (which are common and perfectly legal to have). This was Dad's first knowledge that we had adopted an endangered species, so he asked the breeder whom he needed to contact to make it right.

That's when the breeder convinced Dad that he should give Baque to him (it's illegal to sell an endangered species) because he had all the proper paperwork to keep exotic cats. Intimidated and unsure what to do—it was pretty shocking news after all—Dad made a snap decision to surrender Baque to this man who seemed to have all the answers.

Dad agreed and drove Baque to his new home. It was heartbreaking to say goodbye to our sweet boy, but we knew we couldn't keep him and were assured he'd get the best possible care there. As it turned out, that "goodbye" was a "see you later," but that's a story for another time....

BAQUE'S Lesson: Even in his first few days with us, Baque taught us so many lessons on adaptation and empathy. We did our best to anticipate what he would need and appreciate, to accommodate his natural instincts. The palm trees were a perfect example. It took Dad weeks to build those silly trees, and he went all the way to South Carolina to get the palmetto fronds to crown their tops. Baque definitely showed us again and again it was worth the time and trouble.

When Dad built the indoor/outdoor habitat, we experienced the same lesson at a deeper level. It was incredibly tedious learning what the government agencies required in order to legally house a jungle cat, and even harder to build the habitat to their specifications. But we did it for Baque. That's just what you do for those you love.

3

TIPPYTOES

Deer are not traditionally thought of as pets, and for good reason. Their razor-sharp hooves are murder on indoor flooring. But under the right conditions, a deer can be a pretty special family member. Our pet deer entered our lives quite unexpectedly at the end of one long, hot summer day. I was in the fifth grade and my sister, Lora, had just started high school.

When both your parents are schoolteachers, summers take on a whole new level of freedom and fun. We were free to go wherever we wanted, whenever we wanted, for two glorious months every summer. We took lots of trips, but we also loved being home with our many animals on our sweet, small farm.

Ours wasn't a traditional farm with a big, red barn and livestock. Our barn was affectionately called "the goat shed," and our only livestock were a riding horse, several milk goats, and a pet cow so tame she let us ride on her back. The rest of our animals tended to be more unusual.

Summer days were spent swimming—in our pool or, more often, in the large pond behind the house because it had a rope swing. That is, until the snapping turtle in the pond grew big enough to scare us away. We would ride our bikes to our cousins' house and play, or they would ride their bikes to our house to play. We climbed trees, played endless hours of Uno, took care of the animals and just generally had a blast.

Toward the end of one of those long, glorious summer days, we were all sitting on the front porch watching the sky start to turn colors, listening to the crickets start their symphony. We'd had a big dinner and cobbler for dessert.

In the field next to our horse pasture, Mom's Uncle Ray was mowing his hay with one of those spinning drum attachments on the front of his tractor. It was mesmerizing watching those shiny rows of blades spin round and round on that huge drum, leaving a level path behind it as

Uncle Ray expertly turned back and forth, row after row.

He only had a few rows left, and we could tell he was trying to hurry, hoping to finish the field before it got too dark. Suddenly, the tractor stopped in the middle of a row and Uncle Ray hopped down, running to a patch of tall, uncut hay just in front of where the blades had stopped. He called out for Dad to come over, and we all went running to see what he'd found.

As we stopped by the tractor, I noticed a deer standing at the far edge of the field, looking in our direction. It was unusual for deer to stay put once they knew they'd been spotted, but there she was, almost pacing along the fence line.

I understood why when Uncle Ray moved the hay aside to show us a tiny spotted fawn that was curled up on the ground. The blades had stopped just an inch or so from where he lay, and we thought surely he must be injured to stay there so still.

Though we all knew not to touch baby wildlife —because their mothers would often abandon them if they carried the scent of a human—Uncle Ray reached down and checked the fawn for injuries. As soon as he touched the fawn, the mother trotted away from the fence, deep into the woods.

Satisfied that the deer was uninjured, we all retreated to our yard to watch for the mother to return. Even when it was totally dark, she didn't return. We knew the deer—we'd discovered it was a girl—would need her mother to survive the night. And just like that, we adopted a baby deer.

Uncle Ray went home, planning to finish mowing the next day. Dad went over to the hay field to retrieve the fawn and get her settled inside for the night. As usual, he wore his two shirts—an undershirt and a button-down shirt—so he promptly wrapped his shirt around the fawn and lifted her gently into his arms. We walked back home, where our German Shepherd and two small dogs, a terrier mix and a Pekingese, greeted us with lots of barking and sniffing.

Tails were wagging, though, and the dogs were excited to meet their new friend. We very carefully introduced everyone, and within a few minutes they were fast friends. Dad made a bottle for the fawn to drink—we always had baby animal supplies on hand—and she eagerly drank, while her little white tail flicked happily from side to side.

When she finished her bottle and her energy had returned, she started prancing and playing in the yard with the dogs. That's how she got her name, Tippytoes. She looked like she was tippy toeing every step she took, and it was the cutest thing ever.

It was time to go inside for the night, so we made Tippytoes a comfy bed in the living room, and we slept there with her to keep her company and offer her another bottle if she got hungry during the night. We would try again tomorrow to reunite her with her mother.

Before we knew it, the sun was peeking through the curtains, and Tippytoes was ready for her breakfast. Deciding that a hungry fawn was more likely to be taken back by her mother, we headed back to the hay field. We placed Tippytoes in the same spot where Uncle Ray had found her, hid in the tall hay across the field, and waited for her mother to come back.

We didn't have to wait long. She must have stayed close all night because it wasn't long before she approached the fence and made the noise that deer make, as if she were calling to her baby. Tippytoes answered but stayed where she was. Neither seemed willing to come closer. After a long time, the mother called one last time and then retreated back into the woods. Tippytoes cried for her mother, but she never came back. As sad as I was for her, I was also happy that we got to keep her.

In the coming weeks and months, it became more and more impractical to keep a deer in the house. Tippytoes seemed to think she was a dog, prancing and playing just like they did. As she grew, her hooves were doing a number on our linoleum floors, and it was time to find a better solution.

My fifth-grade teacher had come to visit and was so excited to meet Tippytoes. She and her husband lived so far back in the mountains that the road was a country lane with a gate—very private and definitely a safe distance from roads. When Mom commented on needing to find a permanent home for our hooved houseguest, Mrs. Seals promptly said, "We'll take her. She'd love it at our house. All that room to roam."

Mom was delighted, and we were all relieved to know that she would have such a wonderful home in the absolute perfect location. We were invited to visit any time. At my teacher's house, we said a bittersweet goodbye to Tippytoes, promising to visit as soon as she was settled. A few weeks later, we visited and were excited to see how Tippytoes was doing. They showed us the comfortable stall in their barn that was always open for Tippytoes to sleep in when she wanted to, and she had access to a whole field of corn, plus the feed for their live-stock and plenty of fresh water. And she also had her freedom. She was free to roam the woods for miles and miles, but always came home in the evening for play time and snuggles with the family.

We had timed our visit so that she would likely be there when we were. Sure enough, as we stood in the front yard, Mrs. Seals pointed toward the edge of the woods and said, "Here she comes. Tippytoes, come here, come on, girl." And she did. She walked right over, wearing a bright red bandanna around her neck.

The bandanna was there to let hunters know that she was not fair game and was to be left alone. It was a small enough town that everyone knew to watch out for Tippytoes, and she was perfectly safe from hunters, wherever she roamed.

We had a good long visit, and as it started to get really dark, she gave one last nuzzle and headed back to the woods, as if to say, "See you next time."

Tippytoes lived in the woods and barn there for many, many years, bringing her two new fawns to the edge of the woods each spring, as if to introduce them to the family. The first year that Tippytoes brought her fawns to the edge of the woods, the family named them Peanut and Butter. Each year when she brought her new fawns, they stayed at the edge of the woods while she came into the yard for treats and snuggles. When she was finished with her visit, she would return to her fawns, and all three would head back into the woods. She lived a long, full life there in those woods. And we were all so grateful that she was a part of our lives.

TIPPYTOES' Lesson: From Tippytoes, we learned that proper care of wildlife includes allowing them as much freedom as possible to be true to their unique nature. For Tippytoes, that meant finding a home remote enough that she could roam free in the woods to start a family and just be a deer, but with the appropriate amount of support—like a comfy barn stall with an always-open door, a supply of corn for seasons when food in her habitat was scarce, and the love of a nurturing family.

The easier and more fun approach would have been to keep her in the house with us, but for many reasons, that was simply not practical. Don't get me wrong. Dad and I made a pretty strong case for keeping her as a house pet, but even we knew it wasn't best for her. As a mother herself, Mom could see how important it was to give Tippytoes the opportunity of a full life. And she was right. Loving Tippytoes enough to let her live her best life was by far the best outcome for all involved.

How much more should we take this approach with our friends, family and even strangers? Simply put, it's not about you. Step outside yourself and consider what's best for everyone involved in a situation. You just might be surprised what you find.

4

HARRIET

When I hear the term "pocket pets," I always think of Harriet, our pet opossum. Her life with us began on a glorious spring day when we were headed home from church. Dad was a teacher and a pastor, so our Sundays consisted of church, then home for lunch and a long Sunday afternoon nap, followed by a quick dinner, and a return trip to church for the evening service. Not attending was simply not an option. It might seem like a boring day for some, but we loved Sundays, and the time to just relax and enjoy some quality time together as a family. I was in the third or fourth grade at the time, so family time was still pretty fun.

On this particular Sunday, my cousin Todd,

who was just four months younger, had gotten in trouble with me for tapping loudly on the glass face of our wristwatches, not so subtly communicating to Dad that it was time to end his sermon and set us all free. That did not go well for me. I was dreading the lecture I would undoubtedly get as soon as we got home.

Thankfully, Dad got distracted on the way home by something way more interesting. As was pretty common in the countryside, we saw an opossum lying on the side of the road. Most people drive past a scene like that with no more than a passing thought and possibly a touch of sadness for the "road kill." In our family, any animal sighting warranted closer examination, so Dad immediately pulled the car over on the soft shoulder of the gravel road.

Why would we stop for road kill? Simple. Orphaned animals in need. Where there was road kill—especially in the springtime—there was often a litter of orphans nearby who would surely die without a rescuer.

Dad and I approached the opossum carefully, checking carefully where we stepped, in case the babies had been thrown far from the mother. First, Dad checked for a pulse on the mother, in case she could be saved. Sadly, she was long gone, but he did note that based on her belly she appeared to have babies.

We searched all along the roadside and even in the ditch, despite Mom's warnings not to muddy our shoes in the spring mud. Just when we were finally ready to give up, Dad spotted a tiny movement in the tall grass near the flooded ditch. We ran in the direction of the movement, expecting to find a whole bundle of baby opossums. We did see several babies, but only one was moving. We checked them all to see if any could be saved, but it was too late for all but the one.

Using his trademark top shirt—Dad always wore a button-down shirt over an undershirt—Dad scooped up the one survivor, and we rushed home to do all that we could do for her. Dad and I had forgotten all about the watch incident, and we were in full-on animal rescue mode.

As soon as we got home, we made a comfortable nest for Harriet using shredded newspaper stuffed in the front pocket of my sweatshirt. We hoped the warmth and closeness would mimic what she was used to with her mother. Harriet was small enough to fit in the palm of Dad's hand and was also the perfect size to curl up in a shirt pocket for a nap.

While Mom worked on our lunch, Dad made lunch for Harriet. We always kept eyedroppers and tiny baby bottles on hand for situations just like this one, so he mixed up the most nutritious and age-appropriate concoction, and we bottle-fed the cutest baby opossum we'd ever seen.

I'm not sure how we came up with the name Harriet, but we did. And Harriet loved to eat. She adapted quickly and happily placed her little life in human hands. By the time we went back to church that evening—of course she went with us —she was eating heartily, sleeping soundly, and we had fallen head over heels in love with her.

At that point, Mom was probably not too concerned about having a pet opossum in the house because it was so unlikely that an orphaned baby that young—her eyes were barely open— would survive long. Her interest grew, however, in the coming days and weeks as Harriet not only lived, but quickly doubled in size.

Our new baby opossum wasn't very active during the day since she was nocturnal, and we hardly knew she was there except when it was mealtime. We followed Harriet's lead and listened for her cries when it was time to eat. It was hard to miss since she was always in someone's shirt pocket.

As much as I begged, Harriet never got to go to school with me. I suppose Bandit, our pet raccoon, and the snakes I brought for show-and-tell had ruined the chances of any other animal visits. But she loved being a homebody.

As she grew, we learned firsthand what great climbers opossums are, and how much they like small spaces. By the time she was just a few months old, she could go anywhere she wanted to go in the house, and she did. She wasn't a strong jumper, but could climb any fabric or other non-slip surface with ease. She climbed onto the furniture, up the curtains, and up to our shoulder for a ride.

Napping most all of the daytime hours, Harriet's top priority was finding the most comfortable place to nap. Like all opossums, Harriet loved to hang upside down from her long, strong tail. Even as a tiny baby, she would wrap her tail around our finger to hang upside down. As she grew, she liked to hang from the curtain rod or anything else within her reach.

For naps, she liked quiet, dark corners. Behind

the couch was a favorite spot, in closets—Mom loved that one—and in shoes—another frequent surprise for my poor, sweet Mom.

One fall afternoon, we had all arrived home from school (since both Mom and Dad were teachers, we all got home at the same time) and were settled into our afternoon. My sister Lora was practicing for her weekly piano lesson in the living room. I was (supposedly) doing my homework in my bedroom. Dad was outside milking the goats. And Mom was in the kitchen, starting our dinner.

Bored with my homework, I wondered where Harriet could be. So, I set out on a search for her. She was nowhere to be found upstairs, so I went downstairs. When I didn't find Harriet behind the couch, I started to worry. Had she found a way outside?

Mom was busy in the kitchen with pots on the stove, her knife chopping vegetables, the preheated oven beeping, and all the amazing things she did to make a nutritious and delicious meal for us every night. I asked her if she'd seen Harriet, and she said thankfully, she hadn't.

She opened a drawer by the sink to take out a potholder—oven mitt for those of you north of the

Mason-Dixon Line—and time stood still for a moment.

A millisecond after she slid open that kitchen drawer, we found Harriet. Nothing can prepare you for the shock of a half-grown opossum standing up in your kitchen drawer on her back feet, with her front feet up in the air, hissing the most intimidating hiss she could muster. I don't know how Mom managed not to faint. But what she lacked in fainting, she made up for in screaming.

What came out of her mouth in that moment can only be described as her "Bandit scream," and everyone came running. Lora was first from the piano in the living room, followed closely by Dad from the goat shed where he'd been milking. Everyone but Mom died laughing at the sight of Harriet.

We all knew she was totally harmless and was just doing her best to escape in that moment. Mom knew that too, but her reaction was quite different. Her sheer terror lasted until I scooped Harriet into my sweatshirt pocket and hustled her out of the room faster than either of us knew I could move.

My poor Mom. Can you even imagine?

As Harriet grew, she became unhappy in the

house, and Mom became unhappy with her raiding of the kitchen trash can. Even when she didn't need to go out for the bathroom, Harriet would scratch on the door to go out and would stay longer and longer before coming back inside. She would pace nervously at times, as if telling us she'd rather be outside.

Slowly but surely, we realized it was time to give her the freedom she so clearly wanted. Where our raccoon, Bandit, had seemed reluctant to leave, Harriet was not. She seemed to have enjoyed her time with us in the house, but she was equally happy to be free. She was plenty old enough and healthy enough to thrive on her own. We saw her outside often enough to know that she had successfully transitioned back to the wild.

As much as we (I) had enjoyed having Harriet, from that day on, we never again had an opossum for a house pet!

HARRIET's Lesson: As obvious as it may seem, the lesson Harriet taught us was that fear trumps logic. Every. Single. Time. No matter how thoroughly Mom knew that Harriet was harmless, in the moment that she stood up in her kitchen drawer, all of that logic went right out the window.

Fear is powerful. Too often, it trumps hope, love, and yes, logic. As soon as the fear (Harriet) was removed from the moment, Mom was perfectly fine—except for her blood pressure— and logic returned. But in that moment, there was only room for fear.

5

ZIPPER

The day we met Zipper, Dad and I had been outside all afternoon, working with a foal who needed some help nursing from its reluctant mom. I was in the second or third grade at the time, and I was feeling pretty proud of myself because I had just success-fully milked a horse. Yes, you read that right. You can milk a horse. Horses are not aware of this fact, however, and are not at all on board with being milked.

Regardless, the new foal desperately needed the nutrient-dense first milk, known as colostrum, and his mom simply refused to let him near her. It was rare, but from time to time a mother would reject her baby. We had always been able to acclimate the mother and baby, and this case was no different.

Dad tried first to milk our horse, but his hands were too big. Since my hands were small, it was up to me. I was able to extract most of the colostrum, while Dad held the incredibly uncooperative mother by the halter. It was quite risky, and I don't recommend it. I had to stay incredibly focused on my task, which is hard to do when you're trying to steer clear of an angry mama's hooves.

We put the colostrum and some of the milk that followed in a bottle, and the colt drank it. It didn't take long at all for the colt to perk up, and he used his newfound strength to get to know his mother. After a few days of bottle-feeding and horse counseling, she accepted him enough to let him nurse on his own.

When Dad was convinced that the mother had fully accepted her colt and that he was safe with her, we headed inside for a late lunch and for Dad's afternoon nap. We were halfway between the horse pasture and the house when Dad stopped us dead in our tracks.

He silently pointed toward the stack of firewood in the backyard, where I soon saw the cutest baby skunk. It was barely moving, so we slowly approached, ready to help if it was injured or needed medical attention. We edged closer and closer, but the skunk didn't seem at all afraid of us.

If it ever crossed Dad's mind that we might get sprayed by the skunk, he never showed any concern about it. After all, it wouldn't be the first time we'd had to wash skunk spray off, and we had plenty of tomatoes in the garden to get the smell off. The last time one of us had been sprayed, the victim was our terrier mix, Puppitee, who had the poor judgment to stick her nose into a skunk's den. Little did she know the mama skunk was behind her, but she found out as soon as she turned around. It took three long soaks in tomato juice, followed by several baths, to bring her back to normal.

Most people would avoid a slow-moving, seemingly tame skunk, assuming it was rabid. My dad was not most people. Sure, he was aware of the symptoms of rabies and was on full alert in the event the skunk we saw showed any other signs of it. But he wasn't going to let a little thing like rabies keep him from getting a closer look at a skunk.

It was decision time. Was the skunk rabid, or was it an orphan, weak from lacking proper care? Dad decided on the latter and whispered for me to run inside and grab the kitchen trash can. I quietly but quickly did as he instructed and came back with the kitchen trash can, empty and ready for our rescue operation. Fortunately, my sister was on the phone and Mom was busy upstairs, and I grabbed the kitchen trash can without having to explain myself.

Dad carefully placed the trash can on its side about 20 feet in front of the skunk, but still it didn't move. He motioned for me to go to one side, well behind the skunk, while he went to the opposite side. On his signal, we both took one step toward the skunk, moving in the direction of the trash can. We took step after step, edging closer and closer to the skunk. Finally, he started to move a step at a time toward the trash can.

We had put an apple slice in the trash can, and the skunk seemed to have discovered it. He was moving a bit more quickly and was headed directly for the inside of the trash can. Once he was fully inside the trash can, Dad carefully stood it on its base so we could get a closer look. The skunk inside was so small it would have easily fit in one hand.

As the skunk munched on the apple, Dad decided it wasn't rabid after all. Instead, he was convinced it was simply hungry and was most likely just a few months old. If it were this weak and hungry, it must surely be an orphan and that could only mean one thing. We had just gotten our first pet skunk.

Dad was ready for his nap, and our new pet was ready for a lot more lunch. We decided to take him inside, trash can and all, to get him settled. But first, he would need a name. The choice seemed obvious—Zipper. The white stripe down his back did look exactly like a little zipper.

When we came in the back door of the house, Lora was in the living room on the phone with a friend, and Mom was in the kitchen unloading groceries. Mom only saw that we had the trash can and likely never guessed a skunk was inside. Dad went to get Zipper's lunch and told me to wait there with the trash can.

As I listened to Lora chatting with a friend on the phone, I just couldn't resist. I carried the trash can into the living room and motioned for her to look inside. She motioned for me to leave her alone. Phones then didn't have a mute button, so she shushed me silently with a finger on her lips.

Finally—I suppose to get me out of there—she leaned forward to look inside the trash can. At the sight of Zipper, she screamed. I don't think she was scared of Zipper, but she was smart enough to know that skunks inside a house aren't a good idea.

That scream really perked Zipper up. She darted to the corner of the trash can, hunkered down, and sprayed the most potent defense her tiny body could muster. It was plenty.

Immediately, the room—and the entire first floor of the house—was thoroughly permeated with skunk musk. Mom and Dad both came running from the kitchen, and Lora went running upstairs for a shower.

You would think that would have been the end of our life with Zipper, but you'd be wrong. That was just the beginning. That was actually the last time Zipper ever sprayed—in the house or anywhere else, for that matter. After a slow and careful introduction, Zipper was perfectly happy to snuggle in our pocket, a lap, or in a cozy blanket. She wasn't even afraid of two small dogs—a terrier mix and a Pekingese—and roamed around the house freely, going outside to the bathroom when the dogs went.

Zipper's favorite foods were about the same as Bandit's had been. Where Bandit had favored grapes, Zipper's favorite snack was half an apple.

She would cradle it in her hands and munch delicately around the edges until it was all gone.

Dad decided that since skunks were so similar to cats, we should be able to litter train Zipper like a cat. He got some cat litter and put it in a plastic basin to test his theory. It worked! Within just a few days, Zipper had learned to go in the litter box every time without any accidents and without having to go outside as often as the dogs. I never really thought about whether or not skunks were smart, but Zipper definitely was!

About the time we were thinking of having her scent glands removed just in case she ever changed her mind, friends from church came over for dinner and fell head over heels in love with Zipper. Mom was especially keen on the idea of someone else raising the skunk who was like a ticking time bomb in her house. When Dad recognized the undeniable bond between Zipper and our friends, he happily allowed them to adopt her.

It was a match made in heaven, and they gave Zipper a happy, healthy home full of love and laughter, from that day until she eventually died of old age. To this day, I think of Zipper every time I smell a skunk, thankful for the time we had with her and for the love our friends shared so freely with her.

ZIPPER's Lesson: As unlikely as it was for a skunk to fit a family so perfectly, Zipper did. As much as Zipper needed a family, our friends needed to be her family. It just worked. No animal could have been more loved or received better care. Their vet was even willing to treat her, which was rare. Zipper received all the same vaccinations and routine care that a cat would.

This was a case of "don't judge a book by its cover." Zipper had her musk glands intact, but she had been domesticated. To release Zipper to the wild with no survival skills would have meant certain death. It didn't make sense perhaps to have a skunk as a pet, but it worked out perfectly for everyone.

6

GEORGE & EMILY

I had wanted a pet fox for as long as I could remember. To me, a fox seemed like a perfect mix of cat, dog and teddy bear. It wasn't very common to see foxes injured on the road, however, so we had never rescued a fox.

I was around 13 years old when I finally got my chance to have a pet fox—two, actually. Dad loved going to exotic animal auctions to see all the fascinating animals and to discover which of them would make great pets. And I loved going with him. Mom and Lora always came along to make sure we didn't get out of hand with our selections. It's a good thing, too, because we definitely would have come home with a baby bear cub if they hadn't been there.

Any unsavory sellers were quickly identified and removed, so attendance at these events was almost exclusively responsible pet owners who sincerely loved their animals and were committed to responsible care for them.

On this particular occasion, we had come to learn more about Geoffroy's cats, which Dad wanted to add to his Painted Amazon Cat breeding program. Having raised the Geoffroy's cub—Baque —that Dad had brought from Bolivia, we knew the Painted Amazon Cat would be a huge hit in the cat breeding community. We were disappointed to find that none were in attendance, so we comforted ourselves by exploring all the other amazing animals there.

We saw just about anything you'd find in a zoo, plus rescued wildlife and even some more traditional animals. I spent most of my time by a cage containing an orphaned bear cub. He needed a loving home in which to grow a bit before being rehabilitated and released into his natural habitat. Oh, how I begged for that bear cub. Mom wisely drew the line at bears, and so, I finally moved on.

Lora was a few booths further down from me, and I ran when she called, "Beth, you've got to come see these foxes!" Foxes, you say? And they were silver foxes! The pair were quite young and had reportedly been orphaned in the wild. However, we doubted that story based on the looks of the alleged "owner." It was far more likely that they had been trapped. Based on how scared they seemed, their treatment so far seemed questionable too. Now it was an animal rescue.

We quickly went to find Mom and Dad. We found Dad by the pygmy pigs and Mom was looking for the exit. The smells in the event hall were overwhelming, and the noisy combination of animal sounds made the whole scene nearly unbearable.

Dad was excited to meet the foxes and to investigate our concerns about their alleged owner. He introduced himself and asked countless questions, finally communicating with a glance and raised eyebrows in our direction that he agreed with our assessment of the situation.

After making the arrangements to take the foxes, and loading them carefully in our truck, Dad made a beeline to the event organizers. They assured him that they would investigate further and would ensure that all the animals were treated properly.

I wanted to ride in the truck's camper with the

foxes, but that wasn't possible, so we made them perfectly comfortable in their large, padded crate, beside the pygmy goat we'd bought, and off we went toward home.

When we got home it was already dark, so my foxes, whom I'd named George and Emily (I loved the play "Our Town"), spent the night in the basement. The next day, Dad and I started work on their sprawling outdoor habitat. It was summer vacation so we had plenty of time to build, and I had the whole summer to work with George and Emily. We sketched our design first and then added some measurements, made a trip to the hardware store and started working.

While we planned and built their habitat, I spent countless hours researching silver foxes, their behaviors, their diets, and everything we needed to know to make them feel right at home with us. I learned that silver foxes are the melanistic version of red foxes and that silver foxes are more cautious than red foxes. This would definitely be a challenge.

It took a few days to finish, but the habitat was well worth the effort. By the time we were done, it looked like a zoo exhibit. It was tall enough for an adult to comfortably stand inside, and it was spacious enough to walk around freely, even with the space occupied by the huge tree trunk and bushes we had installed. There was a cozy den for George and Emily to hide inside when they needed to feel extra secure, and they had plenty of room to run and climb freely when they needed exercise.

In order to tame them, I knew I needed to spend countless hours inside that habitat with them, so I installed a comfortable chair and some things I would need while inside. I kept a steady supply of their food, plus plenty of fresh produce, ice cubes and frozen juice for a special summer treat, and, of course, I always brought a good book to read.

The first few days that I spent in the habitat, I completely ignored George and Emily, which wasn't hard to do since they never left their den. We had initially placed their food dishes just outside the door of their den, so they could eat without worrying too much about what was beyond that space—which was usually me. On the third day, when I filled their food bowl, I moved it ever so slightly closer to my reading chair. Each day, I moved it a bit closer, until the bowls were halfway between their den and my reading chair.

That day, they didn't come out at all. They waited inside their den until I went inside the house for dinner, and then rushed out to gobble up all the food.

The next day, I left the bowls right in the middle of the habitat, and they stayed right there until George and Emily were comfortable eating there while I sat in my reading chair. That took weeks! By this time, I was spending three to six hours a day in the habitat with them, reading aloud to them (from "Our Town", of course), singing to them, and even napping in my chair. During that time, they saw that I was perfectly at ease with them, and they slowly but surely became comfortable with me.

It was time to teach them that they could trust me up close as well as far away. I started moving their bowls ever closer to my chair, day by day, until one day they were eating from their bowls within reach of my hand while I sat in my chair.

This was incredible! It was so tempting to just reach out and touch these beautiful silver foxes, but I knew too soon a reach would unravel the weeks of work I'd invested in gaining their trust.

Two days later, I sat in my chair beside their empty food bowl. In my lap, I held their food in a

Ziploc bag. I placed just a few pieces of food in the bowl, beginning with their favorite fruits—apples and nectarines—and waited for them to come over. George was first, as always, and he hardly hesitated at all. Emily lingered a bit behind him, trying to figure me out. When he had eaten all of the food, he looked up at me expectantly, well aware that I had lots more food in the bag.

I reached into the bag and withdrew a slice of nectarine, and slowly lowered it toward the bowl. Instead of depositing it in the bowl and removing my hand, I held it in the bowl, not letting go. George didn't seem to mind until he tried to pull it away and felt the resistance of me holding on. He jumped back in fear, but I didn't flinch. I was prepared for this reaction and held the fruit steady in my hand, still in the food bowl.

Slowly, George approached again, this time barely pulling back at all when I didn't let go. He took a little nibble and sat down to examine me while he chewed. Emily approached and sniffed from a distance but wouldn't come close enough to try a bite. Meanwhile, George took a bigger bite, coming uncomfortably close to my fingers, which still held tight to the fruit slice. He seemed to be challenging me, but I wasn't shaken. I had braced for his bite in case it came, telling myself it couldn't be much worse than a cat bite, given the size of his teeth and the strength of his jaw.

When he had finished eating that slice, I rewarded him by placing several pieces in the bowl while I pretended to ignore them completely. Without my hand in the bowl, Emily eagerly came forward and ate beside George, licking the bowl clean.

Each day after that, for about another week, I fed them from my hand a bit more each time, until I was feeding them exclusively from my hand. It was time for the next step.

I swapped my chair for a bean bag so I would be closer to their level for our daily reading sessions. I continued feeding them from my hand, alternately placing their food bowl on my lap while they ate and I read to them.

After a total of probably three to four weeks, I was able to feed them with one hand while scratching between their ears with the other hand. It was a big step. They were as soft as silk and so sweet. They would look up with the softest expression in their topaz eyes. They swished their tails when they saw me coming with their food—like a dog wagging its tail. They sniffed and licked my hand like a dog and even began to play with me. I started bringing a tennis ball with me, and they loved to chase it. Unlike a dog fetching a ball, however, they just stole the balls, hoarding them inside their den like treasure.

With fall came school and my time with them was more limited. They remained tame and looked forward to my visits, but I could tell they weren't really happy there. Too tame to be released into the wild, and too wild to live in the house safely with our dogs, they needed a home where they could be center stage, with an attentive owner who would love them and care for them as I had.

We asked around at church and school, eventually finding the perfect home. A single, middle-aged man living nearby had always wanted a fox, and had a great deal of experience with rehabilitating wildlife. He even had an extra room in his home that he was eager to convert to an indoor habitat for George and Emily.

As sad as I was to see them go, I could see how happy the man was to welcome them into his home. We checked in on them from time to time just to be sure they were properly cared for, and they always seemed happy and healthy.

.   .   .

GEORGE & EMILY's Lesson: It was years later that I learned the lesson George and Emily were teaching me that summer. I learned that as noble as my idea had seemed, to tame these majestic creatures was a vain and selfish endeavor which benefited me far more than them. In hindsight, I should have rehabilitated them to a healthy condition, without overcoming their fear of humans. Then I should have released them to the wild in a secure area where they could be protected.

How often and how easily we make selfish decisions, focused on the here-and-now and not the long-term benefits for everyone involved. George and Emily had a happy life, but I always wondered what their life in the wild would have been like.

I also learned infinite patience. During those long weeks of spending hours each day inside their habitat, I had lots of time to reflect on things, learning more from George and Emily than I ever taught them.

7

FATUNIA & PETUNIA

P igs? Nothing about pics intrigued us when Dad presented his new "pet" project to the family. We had owned so many different types of animals, and they were all so interesting. We'd had our share of wildlife, including deer, opossum, skunk, foxes, squirrels, and more. And our exotic pets were even more interesting. So, we couldn't believe he was pitching the idea of pigs. Pigs were smelly and boring, right? Wrong.

What Dad wanted were called African Pygmy Pigs, also known as Guinea Hogs. It's a fascinating breed, especially if you're interested in homesteading. My friend, Cathy Payne, published a fantastic history of the breed, titled "*Saving the*

Guinea Hogs: The Recovery of an American Homestead Breed" and I highly recommend it for more detailed information on the breed.

We discovered the breed during the time that Vietnamese Potbelly Pigs had captured the hearts of so many, and Dad saw several advantages when comparing the two breeds. African Pygmy Pigs were much smaller and more petite than Vietnamese Potbelly pigs. They had shorter bodies, so there were fewer issues with their backs and hips, less joint strain, and he believed they were even smarter than their Vietnamese counterparts.

Most everything Dad had assumed about them proved to be true, except for the smell. A pig is a pig and—let's face it—pigs stink. They. Really. Stink. But it was worth it! On our almost eight acres of land, Dad had chosen a large area in the lower pasture, in a well-shaded area near the fence line, for the pig sty. It was as far from the house as possible, to minimize the smell, and it was plenty big enough to accommodate as many as 30 pigs.

The pigs came along when I was in high school. By then, Lora had married her husband, Mike, and wasn't around for as many animal adventures. But Mike was a good sport and went along with Dad's crazy schemes, and they did their best to keep Dad from doing anything too risky. At least they tried. In this case, they both went with Dad to a small Georgia town called Cedartown to buy our first African Pygmy Pigs. At any rate, Dad, Mike and Lora came back with a boar and three unrelated sows—a modest investment into this new venture. But we knew how quickly pigs multiply, so four seemed plenty enough.

Dad, Lora and Mike were excited to introduce us to the newest family members. All of them were affectionate and loved to be petted, but their absolute favorite was a good scratch behind the ears. Within hours of settling into their enclosure in the lower pasture, our pigs had wallowed out a nice deep indention in the dirt, which they rolled around in to cool off. Whether it was dry, as it was that first day, or muddy, as it was most of the time, the pigs loved to roll around in the dirt or mud to cool off.

We named them all, but the only name I clearly remember is a sow named Fatunia. She was my favorite and by far the sweetest. From the very first day, she was the first to come when we called, "Suey!" and the last to leave when we came down for a visit.

As luck and pig husbandry would have it, it

wasn't long at all before our sows had gained enough weight to convince us that piglets would soon join the family. Not just one, or two, but all three sows were expecting. The first two sows delivered within weeks of each other, as Fatunia kept getting rounder and rounder.

Every day we checked for the signs of labor, and every day we were disappointed. Fatunia seemed even more anxious about how long it was taking, as her belly almost touched the ground when she walked. She had nearly stopped walking, mostly just shuffling from where she slept to the food and water and back again.

One Saturday afternoon, my cousin Todd had come over to play. At the top of our list was checking on Fatunia. We wanted to see some more piglets! We eagerly ran down through the pasture with our hands stuffed with carrots and apples for the pigs. We were almost all the way to the pig pen and still didn't see Fatunia. Where could she be?

At the fence, we called her name, and she didn't come. Maybe she was inside the shelter Dad had built for them. Fatunia's portion of the enclosure was separate from the other pigs, to protect her and her new piglets for the birthing process. We opened the gate and went in, expecting her to run out of the shelter, sniffing for the treats we'd brought. Instead, the other pigs crowded against the fence, eagerly calling for them instead. Todd went to the fence to share some treats with the sows there while I ducked into the shelter to look for Fatunia.

There she was, lying on her side, breathing hard and groaning in pain. Todd tossed the rest of the apples and carrots to the other pigs, and we ran to get Dad. Fatunia needed our help, and it couldn't wait another minute.

Dad was napping, as was his afternoon habit. Normally, we were under strict orders not to wake him up from a nap, but we knew an animal emergency qualified. We ran in the front door, panting and sweating, and shouted in unison, "Come quick! Fatunia needs help!" Normally, Dad wakes up slowly and requires at least a cup of instant coffee to come fully awake and ready to function. But that time, he was instantly fully alert and ready to respond.

He slipped on his shoes and told us to go stay with Fatunia while he gathered his supplies. We immediately obeyed and ran as fast as we could back to the pig pen. Fatunia hadn't moved and looked to be in even more distress than when we'd left her. She was clearly in pain.

Dad came down close behind us with his medical supplies and an armful of old towels, arriving in a full run. Our first order of business was to get Fatunia out of the shelter and into the open so we could assess her condition better and perform whatever procedures were needed. It took all three of us to accomplish it, but we were successful. With her heartrate slowing, gums pale, and eyes rolling back in her head, we quickly determined that Fatunia was in shock, and we would lose her if we couldn't quickly deliver her piglets.

Todd volunteered to stay by her head and monitor her vitals while Dad and I worked at the business end of the birthing process. A quick examination told Dad all he needed to know. In addition to being well past the due date, the first piglet was breach and would have to be physically turned in the birth canal before the others could be delivered. There was still movement in her abdomen, so we knew at least some of the piglets were still alive. There was hope.

Dad's hands were too big to turn the breach

piglet, so I took a turn—literally—and was able to reorient the errant piglet for delivery. By this point, Fatunia was barely conscious—and Todd wasn't far behind—so she wasn't strong enough to help us. With my hand in the birth canal, I could feel the next contraction and was able to pull at the same time, so together it was enough to remove the first piglet. Just a few minutes behind that first piglet, which wasn't showing signs of life, two more quickly came, and we could still see movement in Fatunia's belly.

Todd and I had our hands full toweling off the piglets, which were coming out almost faster than we could keep up with. Each one got toweled off with a vigorous back-and-forth motion on the chest and belly to stimulate their breathing. We placed the squirming piglets by Fatunia's sweet face, hoping that the smell of her babies would somehow rouse her back to consciousness. It didn't work. Since her milk had already come in, we did get the piglets to nurse, providing them the nutrient-dense colostrum they so desperately needed.

Meanwhile, Dad was still working frantically to deliver the remaining piglets. After the first piglet, which was breach, and then three more that quickly followed, the fourth piglet was too large to pass through the birth canal. Even with my small hands, I could feel that the size of the fourth piglet was just too large to fit.

With Fatunia barely hanging on and a hopelessly stuck piglet—and more behind it—we had a big decision to make. Dad had a quick consult with Todd and me, proposing that we perform a Caesarean Section to retrieve the remaining piglets. We asked how risky it would be for Fatunia, and he made it abundantly clear that she would likely not survive either way. If we did nothing, both she and her remaining piglets would be lost. If we attempted the C-Section, we could likely save her piglets, and Fatunia would at least have a chance at surviving. What he wasn't telling us was that he had already made the decision and was simply looping us in as an opportunity to learn critical thinking skills and a host of other life lessons that day.

We were in favor of the option that saved the most lives and that was the C-Section. So, he told us where to find the surgical supplies we'd need and instructed us to run as fast as we could to the house, but to be careful not to run on the way back because we'd have sharp objects.

We were on a mission. Almost before Dad

finished giving us instructions, we had turned and started running toward the house, reminding us of the items we were supposed to bring back for the surgery. Before we'd gotten even halfway to the house, we were heard a loud boom. Growing up in the country, everyone recognizes the crack and boom of a pistol shot, and that was definitely what we'd heard.

In an instant we knew that we'd been duped. Dad was simply sending us away to save us from the humane but emotionally shocking ending of Fatunia's life. Farm life is tough, and there comes a time when the kindest course of action is the immediate and painless end. In this case, Fatunia had already lost consciousness—so she felt no pain—and Dad knew there was no way she could be saved. Even so, he didn't want her to be around for the saving of the remaining piglets.

As soon as we heard the shot, we stopped in our tracks, stared at each other in recognition and disbelief, and then ran back to Fatunia as fast as we could. Dad had timed the gunshot so that he had time to cover Fatunia's head with one of the towels so we wouldn't have to see her present condition. He had not, however, covered the incision, where he had indeed performed a C-section.

We arrived just in time to take the last three piglets as Dad handed them to us for toweling, and in some cases, resuscitation. The fourth piglet, which was so large he necessitated the C-Section, was stillborn, but we saved the two which would have followed him out of the birth canal.

In the end, we had saved four of the six piglets, and we had learned that given the size of the fourth piglet, there was no way Fatunia would have survived the delivery. If Dad hadn't acted when he did, we would have lost Fatunia and three piglets. As it was, we had four healthy piglets, who would all grow up to share Fatunia's extra-sweet personality.

It's hard to describe how cute these piglets were. At less than half the size of a normal piglet, these little guys and gals had shiny, pink snouts and soft black hair. It would become coarse and almost bristly in adulthood, but for now it was silky soft. The piglets got extra attention every morning when brought their food and every afternoon as soon as we got home from school. They loved to snuggle almost as much as they loved to eat.

With two other nursing sows, we were able to "adopt" Fatunia's piglets into other, slightly older, sibling units. The exception was one extra-sweet piglet who reminded us so much of Fatunia. We had named her Petunia and bottle-fed her.

Petunia got to spend a little while as an indoor pig while she was being bottle-fed. It was easy to see why the Vietnamese potbelly pig was sweeping the nation as a pet craze. Pigs (when miniature) make fantastic pets! Within just a day or two of being an indoor piglet, Petunia had learned most of our dogs' basic commands—including come, sit, stay and lie down—and she had even learned to play fetch with a ball. Her hooves didn't get very good traction on the linoleum floors, but she was still pretty fast. And, best of all, we got to see glimpses of Fatunia every day in our sweet Petunia.

Fatunia's Lesson: It took a long time for Todd and I to accept the lesson we learned the day that we lost Fatunia and gained Petunia because we were focused on the losing and not the gaining. When we heard that gunshot, we were so angry with Dad —that day and for a long while later—for summarily deciding to end Fatunia's life. We were so mad that we failed to recognize that he had made the decision that yielded the greatest gain with the least amount of loss possible. He explained it to us as "the circle of life," assuring us that their mother's death was the only way the piglets could have lived. Quite literally, her death gave them life, thus "the circle of life."

It wasn't an easy decision, and it was so hard to lose a pet we so dearly loved, but in the end, Dad was right. And that lesson from Fatunia of greater gain has served us all well from that day forward.

8

BOOMER

By the time I started high school, we had cared for all sorts of different animals, from wildlife to animals you'd find in a zoo. And we named every single one. When guests at our home visited, they often asked how we came up with the name "Boomer" for our male ostrich. It usually wasn't long before Boomer showed them himself how he earned his name, by making the loud, booming noise he typically made when he came to the fence for a quick pat on the back or for his food and water.

Technically, our "ostriches" were called rheas, a variety of South American ostrich that are just a bit smaller than traditional ostriches and have less flashy coloring. Ours were a dull grayish, tannish color and were known to be more affectionate than ostriches. But one thing was the same—both ostriches and rheas are as dumb as a box of rocks.

It's been said of turkeys that if you leave them out in a heavy rain they can drown because they don't have sense enough to lower their head to keep the water from pouring into their lungs. I think the rheas could have given those turkeys a run for their money.

We learned of their limited intelligence the hard way when we nearly lost a herd of hatchlings due to gluttony. They literally lacked the sense to stop eating when they were full. But first, I'll tell you how we got the eggs in the first place.

Boomer was our only male in the herd because males tend to be aggressive with other males. And Boomer definitely had a dominant personality. He was aloof and distant compared to the dozen or so females we had in the herd. And he was particularly troublesome when he was sitting on a nest full of eggs.

Yes, you read that right. Unlike other poultry, which predominantly relies on the female for birth and parenting duties, ostriches (and rheas) reversed the roles. Gender equality was the name of the game with Boomer. All the female ostrich (hen) had to do was lay the eggs and walk away. The male ostrich (rooster) would then guard the nest, sit on the nest until the chicks hatched, and then raise the chicks to adulthood.

As you might imagine, Boomer took his job quite seriously, flying into an immediate rage whenever anyone—even one of the mothers—approached his nest. My dad always had a tendency to do things the hard way and to get what he wanted regardless of risk, so he eagerly accepted the challenge of robbing Boomer's nest.

Why didn't he just leave the eggs to hatch naturally? There were several reasons, but primarily it was because ostrich chicks were known to require a little extra assistance to make it past the early stages of growth. We had set up a large, well-equipped enclosure specifically for this purpose, with heat lamps, comfortable bedding and everything an ostrich chick could need to get the best possible start in life.

Secondary to the welfare of the chicks was Dad's desire to use the stillborn eggs for art projects. An ostrich egg is exceptionally hard, able to withstand up to 500 pounds of vertical pressure without cracking. That allows the egg to bear the weight of an adult ostrich sitting on it for the almost two months required to hatch. It also allows for some pretty incredible artwork in the hands of skilled artist with a Dremel tool.

My dad was quite an artist, proficient in music, painting and—apparently—egg art. Whenever we found a stillborn egg, he used an electric drill to blow the contents of the egg out until it was completely empty and clean inside (thanks to a generous rinse in bleach water). Then he would pencil sketch an intricate scene on the egg—often a beach or mountain landscape—over which he would apply the Dremel to etch the design directly into the eggshell. The effect was stunning. At about six inches long, there was plenty of space to fill with the scenes Dad engraved there.

One of the first times we robbed Boomer's nest, we cooked the egg just like a scrambled chicken egg, because why not? Since each egg weighed from three to five pounds, one egg equaled roughly the equivalent of two dozen chicken eggs. Far more nutrient dense than chicken eggs, the yolk was a deep orange color, and the flavor was exceptionally rich. But for the most part, all of the eggs we took hatched into healthy adults.

The most entertaining part of it all was the actual act of robbing the nest. We took lots of precautions because Boomer could run so fast—up to 45 miles per hour—and was armed with a long middle toe capable of ripping through skin with a single strike. Safely robbing the nest took about eight people.

Basically, we formed a huge circle around the perimeter of the pasture where the ostriches were, each armed with a long stick of some sort—some had brooms, some had tree branches—and slowly closed in toward the nest. The plan was to draw Boomer's attention from one to the other while Dad robbed the nest.

Dad wasn't part of the circle. He was hidden in the bushes slightly closer to the nest, ready to dart to the nest as soon as Boomer moved far enough away from it. He had a canvas bag slung across his shoulder to collect the eggs.

The "dump nest" as it was called was the central repository for all of the hens to lay eggs in, and it typically had as many as 50 eggs at a time. With each egg measuring six inches long and 3-5 pounds, it took several trips to get them all.

Each time Boomer started to look Dad's way, someone in the circle would get his attention to draw him in their direction instead of Dad's. If Boomer got too close to any one person in the circle, someone on the other side would get his attention. All the while Boomer was strutting in all directions inside the large circle, with his wings extended to their full wingspan and his deep voice booming in an eerily threatening tone.

Once in a while, Boomer caught sight of Dad near the nest, and he had to take safe shelter on the other side of the fence until someone got Boomer moving in their direction instead. The whole event was extraordinarily nerve-racking, and everyone practically ran from the pasture the moment Dad gave the all-clear.

Then it was time to check the eggs to cull any stillborn or double-yolk eggs. They would soon become works of art. The healthy eggs were quickly moved to the hatchling center we'd set up with heat lamps, food and water. That began the arduous task of keeping them on their feet long enough to grow leg bones strong enough to bear their weight without bowing to the point of immobility.

You see, the chicks would eat literally all of the

time without stopping. A few actually ate themselves to death before we realized what was happening and rationed their food. Those who had eaten to the point of immobility were unable to make it to the food and water to stay alive, and would have died if Dad hadn't figured out how to strengthen their bowing legs.

He knew that their leg bones were too weak to hold so much upper body weight, so he designed leg braces with a hinge at the knee joint. He made a variety of sizes so we could refit each bowing leg with a larger brace each time they outgrew the current one. Before long at all, they were all at a healthy weight, and their legs were straight and strong. Crisis averted—at least for the moment. With ostriches, or rheas, there was always the potential for more drama.

Boomer's Lesson: We learned lots of important lessons from Boomer and his brood. From Boomer, we learned how fiercely a parent will defend his or her child. From his chicks we learned that our own selfishness and greed can blind us to the most obvious dangers. I'm sure that none of those gluttonous chicks ever considered that without our help they would have died as a direct result of their own ignorance. I think of those foolish chicks so often when I'm being short-sighted, and they remind me to stop and think beyond the moment and beyond my immediate desires.

9

PUMPKIN

I f you think goats in pajamas are cute, wait until you see a *pygmy* goat. When we got our first few pygmy goats, I was in high school and able to help more with the animals. We had miniature horses and miniature pigs, so it seemed only natural to add pygmy goats to the mix. They were much smaller than our standard-sized goats, but at about half the size of a normal goat, they weren't ridiculously small.

Dad and I were on a mission to find the smallest pygmy goat we could find. Anytime we saw a promising classified ad in the *Exotic Trader* magazine, Dad would call with the same question, "How small is your smallest goat?" We drove from our small Virginia homestead to Kentucky,

Tennessee, Georgia and even further in search of the smallest of the small.

We were amazed by how easily these goats could jump our fence. They practically defied gravity, jumping almost as high as a normal-sized goat. We used wire fencing with large squares, and it came on a roll like you would find chicken wire in a farm store. Each time a new goat was able to clear the fence, we'd add another, higher row.

I can't remember where she came from, but as soon as we saw Pumpkin, we knew we had found what we were looking for. Pygmy goats range in height from 16 to 23 inches at the withers (that's shoulders for you city folk), and Pumpkin was barely 16 inches fully grown. We were thrilled! With Pumpkin and our smallest Pygmy billy goat, we could build the smallest herd anyone had ever seen.

Not only was Pumpkin particularly tiny, she was extra sweet in every way. Goats are known for being cuddly and entertaining, joking and pranking everyone at every opportunity. But Pumpkin was something special. She was smaller than our German Shepherd, Jubilee, whom we called "Jubel," and her favorite thing to do was snuggling. I would walk into the goats' part of the pasture, which ran adjacent to our house for easy mowing, and as soon as I sat down on the grass, there she was. She would lie down right against me, as close as she could get, with her head in my lap for an ear scratch. Like our dogs, she also loved a good belly scratch.

It wasn't long before Pumpkin's belly began to swell, as so many goats' bellies do in the springtime. We could hardly wait to see how tiny her babies would be. We expected a pair, as is most common for goats, but had previously seen as many as four goats born together, so it was always a fun surprise.

As the days and weeks went by, Pumpkin's belly drooped closer and closer to the ground, until it was practically dragging the ground when she walked. It had to be any day now! But there were still no kids. She had less and less energy, and we began to worry. Memories of Petunia's traumatic birth scene came to mind every time I checked on Pumpkin, and we were determined not to let her delivery reach crisis level.

Finally, one beautiful spring afternoon, Pumpkin showed all the signs of imminent labor. We were with her from beginning to end, helping her every step of the way. More than once, we wondered if a C-section would be necessary. Thankfully, it wasn't.

With a great deal of patience and skilled veterinary care, Dad and I safely delivered the tiniest pair of kids we'd ever seen. Pumpkin was weak and took a few days to fully recover, but both she and her kids survived and thrived. They were indeed the smallest pygmy goats we had seen so far. If the goal were to create the smallest ever goats, we must have come pretty close.

After the trauma she'd experienced from her first pregnancy, we decided it wasn't safe to put Pumpkin through the experience again. No matter how much we wanted to see the world's smallest goat, we weren't willing to risk Pumpkin's life to get it. In the end, Dad decided to pass on the pygmy goat opportunity. Pumpkin lived a long, happy life.

Pumpkin's Lesson: Once again, we learned that selfishness has brutal consequences. By focusing on our own goals (world's smallest goat), we inadvertently jeopardized Pumpkin's health. As hard as it was to not risk a second attempt at motherhood, it was the right decision for her, and that was far more important than our own pride and vanity.

10

THE HORSE: PART ONE

Sometimes, despite our best efforts, tragedy could strike our animals that we so dearly loved. I'll tell you right now, this is a sad chapter. If you're a parent, feel free to make up your own story here if your younger audience isn't ready for this.

Ready? Here we go. During my high school years, my favorite animal that we had was, by far, our miniature horses. I'm not sure when they crossed our radar, but the moment Dad and I realized there was such a thing as a miniature horse, we knew we had to have one—or twelve.

We checked the classified ads in the *Exotic Trader Magazine*, went to exotic animal auctions, and even stopped at random strangers' houses if we saw small horses in their pasture. Seriously. That's how we found our best stallion, Tiny Tim.

We were driving through Georgia, to or from a family vacation in Florida, when Dad spotted a whole herd of miniature horses. Of course, we stopped at the house nearest the pasture, knocked on the front door, and asked if we could see their miniature horses. I would never do that now, but that stop turned out to be perfectly providential.

We met the nicest family, and they taught us all they knew about miniature horses. We stayed for what seemed like hours—and maybe it was. Before we left, Dad had bought several horses from them. Since we didn't vacation with an empty horse trailer in tow, the family agreed to deliver the horses to us at home the next week. They were excited to see our other animals anyway.

We learned a lot about miniature horses that day. According to the American Miniature Horse Registry (AMHR), a miniature horse cannot exceed 38 inches at the withers (last hair of the mane). In the "A" division of the AMHR, horses must measure 34 inches and under, compared to the "B" division, which permits horses as tall as 34 to 38 inches.

We picked out a stallion, Tiny Tim, who was

just 29 inches tall and was the most beautiful brown and white pinto I'd ever seen. His mane and tail were so long his tail touched the ground. And he was such a sweetheart, snuggling right up against the fence to get close to us.

And we chose three mares—a beautiful bay (32 inches tall), a sorrel about the same height and a palomino mare who was almost too tall to be a miniature horse. The height limit for the "A" division was 34 inches and that's what she was, but she was stunning. Her coat was golden with a rich, almost caramel color, and her mane and tail were the purest cream color and so silky. I'd always had a weakness for palomino horses, and her personality was just remarkable. Tall or not, I had to have her.

Always the entrepreneur, I asked Dad if I could be in charge of the miniature horse project, and he agreed. I even wrote up a contract when we got home, stating that I would get half of every dollar earned and that I would do half the feeding, stall cleaning and veterinary work. I held him to the profit portion of the contract, but he graciously didn't enforce the shared labor and expense portion of the contract. It was a great lesson in investment as well as contract negotiation.

Sometime the next week, a horse trailer pulled into our driveway, carrying precious cargo. We were all so excited to watch our four new miniature horses explore our pasture and barn, meeting our red heeler, Gypsy, who couldn't help but try to herd them.

Gypsy and Tiny Tim were fast friends and played together like two dogs would, having a grand time and even lying down beside each other in the field when they were tired of prancing and playing tag.

As the summer went on, I spent hours outside every day, just brushing, training and snuggling our horses. They were so tame that if I sat down in the pasture, they would come trotting over to lie down beside me like a dog would. It was amazing!

As pretty as the palomino mare was, my favorite was the bay, whom we had named Becky. For the non-horse folks out there, a bay is that rusty red color all over with a black mane and tail —and sometimes black on their legs. When there's color on a horse's legs, it's calls socks or stockings, depending how high on the leg the color goes. Becky was a beautiful bay and she was the sweetest, gentlest mare and was always the first to run to the fence to greet me after school.

When we realized Becky was expecting her first foal, I was over-the-moon excited, checking on her all the time. Dad was excited because Tiny Tim was an amazing sire, at just 28 inches tall, and he was expecting an amazing—and valuable—foal from this pair. Tiny Tim was so small that I could stand over him with both feet on the ground. Imagine a fully-grown horse so short it can walk right through your legs.

When she looked so big she could pop, I checked on her every morning before I left for school, and every afternoon when I got home. I was usually the one who helped all the animals deliver their babies because my hands were smaller than Dad's, and he'd taught me how to deliver baby animals when I was just five years old. In fact, he would wake us up in the middle of the night to see an animal give birth. It was a magical experience and incredibly educational.

The first time that I remember Dad waking us up to be there for a live birth was late one night— in the middle of the night—when I was five or six years old. Lora and I were reluctant to leave our warm beds to set in the cold of early spring watching and waiting for what could be hours. But we grabbed our matching quilted housecoats and fuzzy slippers to follow Dad out to the goat shed.

It was so cold we could see our breath as we entered the goat shed. It was surprisingly warm inside with all the hay stacked along the walls for insulation and scattered on the floor of the "birthing suite" for the doe's comfort. On the floor was one of our mama goats, with her sides heaving in and out with each contraction stronger than the one before it.

In hindsight, I'm pretty sure she didn't need any help at all, but Dad wanted us to be part of the process, so he showed us how to feel for the kid's head and front hooves to be sure they were in the right position for delivery. He cautioned us to make sure the head was down and not angled away from the hooves so it could get stuck.

We anxiously watched for the tiny white front hooves to emerge so we could get a good grip and "help" the mother deliver her precious cargo. As much as Dad had cautioned us to hold on really tight to the front legs so we didn't fall backward, I lost my grip and did exactly that. I fell straight back into a pile of what we called "goat pills" or manure. Not a happy camper, I stood up and planted one foot close to the mother and the other far enough behind me to not slip again.

That's the exact moment the goat peed on my favorite pair of fuzzy slippers. Lora was watching from a nearby hay bale and laughed until she cried, along with Dad. I didn't laugh at all. When the baby was out, we helped the mom clean it up so it could stand on wobbly hooves to nurse. Dad asked me what I wanted to name the kid since I was to the one who helped deliver her. Without a moment's hesitation, I declared her name would be "Peepee-Shoes," and so it was.

Now with a decade of experience helping animals deliver their babies, I thought I was ready for anything. One afternoon, Dad and I saw Becky lying on her side when we pulled into the driveway. This was it—she was ready! We left everything in the car and ran to her side. When we got closer, we could see that her legs had gotten tangled in the barbed wire fence—so badly tangled that she couldn't stand. She had delivered her foal, but she couldn't move enough to clear the mucous from its nose so it could breathe.

I'll spare you the details, but suffice it to say her legs were cut from the barbed wire, her breathing was shallow from going into shock, and the foal was inside the mucous membrane and not moving.

Dad took charge of stabilizing Becky, and I ran to the foal to see what could be done to save it. I tore open the amniotic sac and frantically wiped away mucous from its nose, rubbed its sides to stimulate its heart and lungs and even attempted chest compressions and rescue breathing—yes, CPR on a horse—but it had been too long.

That's when I noticed the color. The little filly was the most beautiful and perfect palomino. I told Dad it was such a shame to lose such a beautiful palomino, and I switched my focus to Becky, who was starting to stabilize under Dad's care. I quickly worked to free her legs from the fence and then got the supplies to treat the cuts on her legs.

Finally, she was able to stand on unsteady legs and walked over to where we'd placed her baby gently on the grass. It was pure heartbreak watching her nuzzle her stillborn filly, and I said again what a shame it was to bury such a beautiful horse.

Becky went on to live a long and happy life with us and had other foals. But there was always a special place in our hearts for her first lost filly.

Little did I know, I had not seen the last of that beautiful filly.

BECKY's Lesson: For reasons you'll better understand in my next book, *Never Hide a Horse in the Freezer*, Becky taught me that you have to be very careful what you say. A passing comment for one person can be interpreted by another person as having much more weight than was intended. We also learned that no matter how hard you fight to save something, sometimes it's just not enough. It was all I could do to walk away that day, knowing that Becky would live on but her filly was gone. But Dad reminded me of the frailty of life and that we should savor every moment as if it's our last.

11

ANGEL

Some kids get cash to celebrate their college graduation. Some get a job. I got an alpaca. Believe it or not, an alpaca wasn't even the most unusual gift Dad ever gave me. More on that later.... Don't feel bad for me, though. It was actually a pretty awesome gift because it translated to several thousand dollars when we eventually sold the herd.

Dad was practical that way, which is surprising because in most things his logic doesn't make sense to anyone else. He thinks on a different plane from most folks, and this has a delightful, eccentric effect with an always surprising result.

In this case, he had realized an incredibly lucrative opportunity to help finance his missions work in Bolivia, while also improving the vitality and genetic profile of the American alpaca population. When he learned that alpacas had not been imported from Bolivia in a few decades, he looked into the benefits of raising alpacas. He was charmed by their sweet personality and had all sorts of ideas for using the alpaca wool. He also saw dollar signs.

In Bolivia, the going rate for an alpaca at the time was about $35. In the United States, an alpaca could sell for as much as $10,000. Even a lower quality alpaca would net at least $5,000, and that was in the early 1990s. By Dad's reasoning, he could buy an entire herd of alpacas in Bolivia, hand-picking those with the best dispositions, the highest quality, and the sturdiest health. Even with the high cost of quarantine, he would make an enormous profit and would enrich the U.S. breeding program at the same time. It was a win-win. And the profits he planned to re-invest in his missions work in Bolivia. So, technically, it was a win-win-win.

The prospect of figuring out the process for international export of livestock would be daunting for most people, but Dad was not most people. He loved a challenge, and he loved learning new things – this was definitely both. While in Bolivia, he lived at sea level, down in the rainforests of southern Bolivia, and the alpacas lived on the Altiplano in northern Bolivia near the capital city of La Paz.

So, Dad set out for La Paz, another 24-hour bus ride up from the Amazon rainforest on the "Road of Death." Once in La Paz, Dad quickly set up trips to local homes on the Altiplano, also called El Alto, to scout out the best alpacas. The owners were delighted when he paid them so generously for their best alpacas, so he helped families along the way, a little more with each alpaca he purchased.

As his herd grew day by day, he rented a comfortable space for their care and feeding there in Bolivia, enlisting the help of a veterinarian to vaccinate each alpaca and ensure they were free of communicable diseases. They would still have to stay in a quarantine facility in the U.S. upon entry, but this was the required process to safely and legally export them.

Once he had gathered all the alpacas he needed, almost 20 in all, Dad made arrangements to travel with his alpacas to the USDA-authorized quarantine facility in New York, where he would pay room and board for each alpaca for the several months they would stay there. At the end of the quarantine period, the USDA released the herd into our care, and somehow Dad transported them all from New York to our small family farm in rural Virginia.

That is when he called me at college to tell me that he had my graduation present and that it was an angel. After 18 years in this family not much surprised me—even his announcement that he was giving me an angel. He had chosen what he thought was the best quality, best-dispositioned alpaca in the herd, and gave her to me as a graduation present. He had named her Angel because of her sweet disposition and her snow-white coat.

To this day, Angel remains the most expensive gift I've ever been given by anyone. I suspect that will always be true. When another alpaca breeder heard that Dad had imported his herd directly from the best stock in Bolivia, he jumped at the chance to buy the entire herd. I suspect the descendants of those alpacas remain among the highest quality in the nation.

True to his word, Dad re-invested the profits from the sale into his missions work in Bolivia. That project funded many more years of life-changing education, nutrition, adoption, housing, and other projects, including a television station, a radio station, an orphanage, a feeding center, and so much more. And no one can ever top my answer to the question, "What's the most unusual gift you ever got?"

ANGEL's Lesson: Considering how many families in need she supported, I suppose Angel the alpaca really was an angel, as she and her friends did a whole lot of good for a whole lot of people. And they got the best possible care and a very loving home in the process.

Dad's idea to import an entire herd of alpacas from another continent sounded totally illogical to everyone because it was so much work and so unorthodox. He had to travel from farm to farm in Bolivia for weeks to find the right alpacas, had to figure out all the insane logistics to transport them each step of the way, had to pay for several months of quarantine, and so much more.

Why did he do it? I think he saw an opportunity that everyone had dismissed as not viable, and he simply willed his plan to work. He wasn't afraid to try something new and fail at it. He just knew he had to fail forward. And he did.

He made mistakes along the way, but he learned from them all and, in the end, he did it. He single-handedly earned tens of thousands of dollars to support his life's work in Bolivia. And that's not nothing.

EPILOGUE

Did you notice some hints about future stories— foreshadowing—in a few of those chapters? If you got the feeling that there was more to some of those stories, you're right. To hear the exciting conclusion of Baque's and Becky's stories, and much more, check out the final book of the "Never" series, titled *Never Hide a Horse in the Freezer*, available everywhere November 2019.

In the final book of this trilogy, you'll meet some of the pets my dad and his dad had as children, as well as how my animal-centered childhood shaped my current family's pet preferences.

To get the latest updates, join my mailing list at:

http://bethdetjens.com

Until then...

Never put an alligator in your car.

Made in the USA
Middletown, DE
21 November 2021